WE CARRY KEVAN

KEVAN CHANDLER

ILLUSTRATED BY NATALIE PETERSON

Kevan was a whiz on wheels.

But sometimes, he wished he had wings.

If he had wings, he could go up, up, up,
on the shoulders of the wind.

He could be free as a bird—
free to see the whole world.

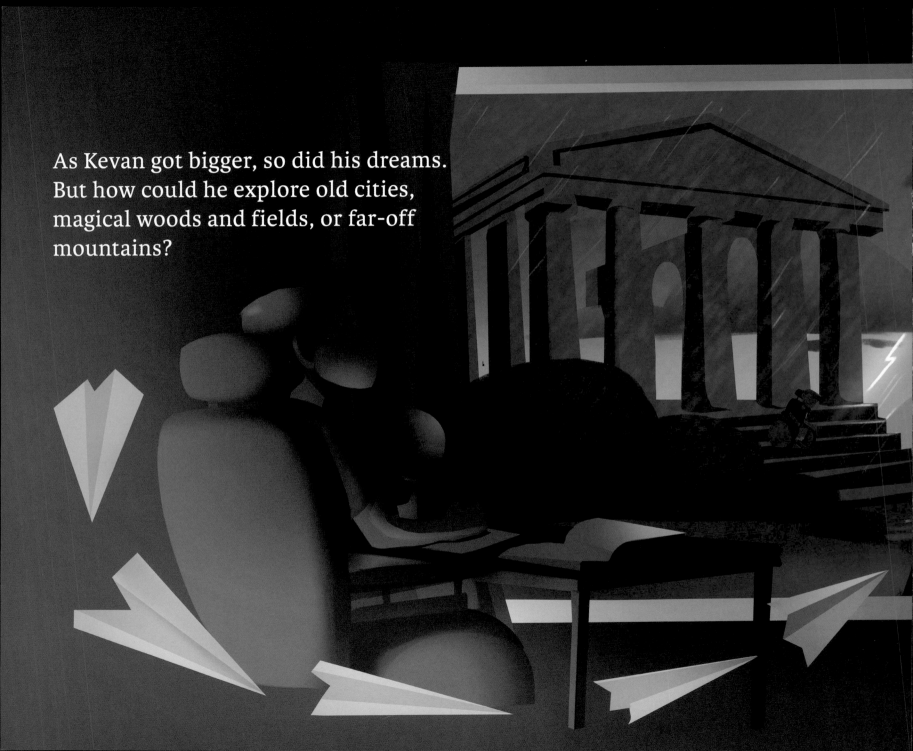

As Kevan got bigger, so did his dreams. But how could he explore old cities, magical woods and fields, or far-off mountains?

There were too many places
his wheels couldn't go.

One day, Kevan's friends said,
"We're going on an adventure.

And you're coming with us...
in this backpack."

But Kevan said...

WHAT IF WE GET BLOWN OFF A CLIFF?

"Trust us," said Tom.

And Kevan did.

Kevan and his friends explored the world

At night, Paris was full of jingles and jangles.

All the jiggling jolted Kevan in his backpack, but his friends noticed.

"Let's get you more comfortable," said Robbie. "Dancing is all about feeling good, after all."

In London, Kevan asked the birds, "What does it feel like to ride on wings?"

"What does it feel like to ride in a backpack?" they sang back.

They journeyed into magical woods.

"Be careful of those roots!"
Kevan said to Ben's feet.

"Trust me," said Ben.

And Ben's feet carried them safely through.

At the top of a hill, Tom took off the backpack and set it on the ground.

"You're not just going to leave me here, are you?" said Kevan as Tom walked away.

"Trust me," said Tom.

And Kevan got to enjoy a quiet
moment to himself in the
wide open world around him.

They still had a mountain to climb, though.
It whispered to them, "Bring it on."

Kevan wasn't so sure they could,
but his friends felt differently.

"Trust us," they said one more time.

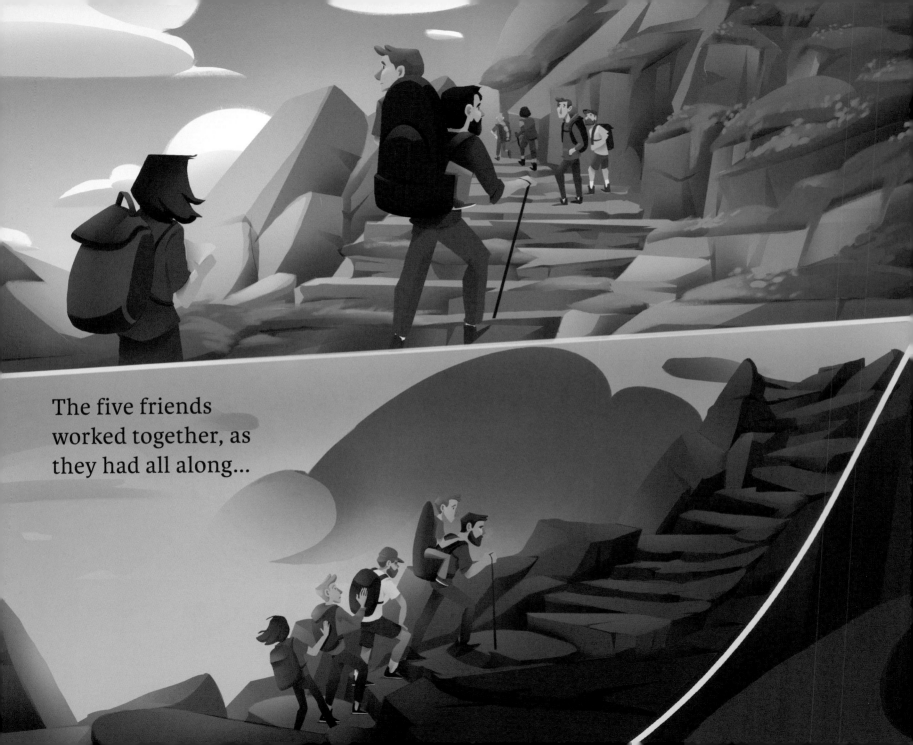

The five friends
worked together, as
they had all along...

Looking out for each other and trusting each other to help, care, and catch.

In a place where wheels could never go,
Kevan went up, up, up, soaring on the
shoulders of his friends.

Free as a bird.

Free to see the world.

About the Author

Kevan Chandler grew up in North Carolina and has a disease called spinal muscular atrophy, type 2, that makes him not be able to walk. An avid storyteller, he has written several books, including a grown-up memoir of his adventures, also entitled *We Carry Kevan*. He travels and speaks worldwide about his super cool friends and unique life with a disability. Kevan is also the founder of a nonprofit organization, which is called (you guessed it!) We Carry Kevan. He and his wife, Katie, live in Fort Wayne, Indiana, where they enjoy growing vegetables, making homemade bread, and reading to each other.

About the Illustrator

Natalie Peterson is a skilled kung fu master and expert unicorn tamer. Just kidding, she is a background painter and illustrator who lives in Nashville, Tennessee with her very cool husband and very cool baby. Most days you can find the three of them making art and riding the unicorn Natalie tamed.

WE CARRY KEVAN

http://wecarrykevan.org

What is "We Carry Kevan"?

In the summer of 2016, Kevan and his friends took a trip across Europe. They left his wheelchair at home, and his friends carried him for three weeks in a backpack. "We Carry Kevan" was the name of their campaign to raise funds and awareness about the trip. Because of the overwhelming positive response from families with disabilities through the campaign, We Carry Kevan (WCK) was established as a 501c3 nonprofit organization. The mission: to mobilize individuals with disabilities by redefining accessibility to be a cooperative effort. People helping people.

The board, staff, and volunteers of WCK seek to foster a culture of creative accessibility by collaborating with families with disabilities around the world - sharing Kevan's story to encourage and inspire, traveling to visit them in their homes and communities, distributing specially designed carrier backpacks, and having ongoing conversations about friendship and new or alternative ideas for customized access.

What is the WCK Backpack?

The WCK Backpack was initially designed as a personal adaptation of the Deuter Kid Comfort 3, for Kevan and his friends to use in Europe. Since then, We Carry Kevan has partnered with Deuter to further develop the WCK Backpack, with additional adjustable pads, straps, and accessories for customized comfort and support. This backpack is specially designed to carry individuals with mobility-related disabilities so they can go where wheelchairs cannot, with the help of friends and family.

We Carry Kevan provides a user manual and tutorial video, and offers personal consultations to help customize adjustments for unique situations. Additionally, families can request financial assistance for a backpack through the WCK Causes Program.

How can you be involved?

- Purchase a WCK Backpack for yourself or someone you love
- Give a monthly or annual donation to support the on-going work of WCK
- Donate to give a sponsored backpack to a family through our Causes Program
- Request a sponsored backpack for yourself or someone you love
- Invite Kevan to speak at an event or share with a group
- Sign up for the weekly e-newsletter from Kevan
- Follow us on social media and share our posts: @wecarrykevan on Facebook, Twitter, and Instagram